A BOOK OF OTHER DAYS

A BOOK OF OTHER DAYS

BY

LISA M. STEINMAN

ARROWOOD BOOKS • CORVALLIS, OREGON

Versions of "A Sort of Spring Song," "Against Things," "Cloning," "Lost Souls," "Hum-Drum Days," "Looking Forward to Looking Back," "The Pleasures of Merely Recirculating," "Rosaries," and "Coming Up for Air" first appeared in *Nimrod,* having won the Pablo Neruda Prize. "The Passion For Imitation Tries" appeared in *The Webster Review.* "Hearing Voices" appeared in *Backbone.* "Spring's Eternal " and "The Inner Man" first appeared in *Fine Madness.* "Biology Lesson" first appeared in *Zyzzva.* "The Way He or She Sees It" and "Nautical Gesture" appeared in *The Madison Review.* "Theaters of Operation" appeared in *Ascent.* "Still Life" and "Familiarity" appeared in *Pennsylvania English.* "Exercise For the Heart," "What To Do," and "Signs Of The Times" first appeared in *Northwest Magazine.* "Ground Control" appeared in *Fireweed.* "How to Live Forever" appeared in *Calapooya Collage.*

Cover art, *"Tea and Checkers,"* by Merrilee Rayle.
Designed and typeset at Arrowood Books and ImPrint Services.
Printed in the U.S.A.

Arrowood Books, Inc., P. O. Box 2100, Corvallis, OR 97339

Library of Congress Cataloging-in-Publication Data:

    Steinman, Lisa Malinowski, 1950 -
      A book of other days : poems / by Lisa M. Steinman.
         p.   cm.
      ISBN 0-934847-17-7 (alk. paper : $19.95). — ISBN 0-934847-18-5
      (pbk. : $9.95)
      I. Title.
      PS35569. T3793B66   1993
      811'.54--dc20   92-40012
                                        CIP

For Jim

TABLE OF CONTENTS

HOW TO LIVE FOREVER

On the run again, I will not settle for this world
in which we prowl like tourists looking for a good deal.
I hold on only to memory, like the pear tree which bore one piece of fruit.
We let it go brown on the windowsill, saving it so long.

There are many morals to this story:
pears rot; routine drives us away from home.
The road sign tells us bridges freeze first;
the world is full of solid ground we know we cannot trust.

The old man squatting on the tavern stoop has the hair of a former lover.
Perhaps the objects of memory age too.
To escape myself, I turn to culture. In the theater behind me
everyone maligns their friend Peggy, who takes so much time dressing.

The tour guide suggests the *Duchess of Malfi* is about honor and words,
and is asked his shoe size. He disapproves.
I learned the power of words from Tinkerbell, from Quasimodo,
from a music teacher who pared her nails to Beethoven, saying

"Do not do as I do." Peggy arrives for Act III. She lost her son last year.
She's been shopping through Act I, and the Duchess is pregnant.
Poor Duchess, poor honor. We all hit the pavement together
no matter what size shoes we wear.

The sign in the store window outside the theater
tells the parcel service when to stop. *UPS, YES*, it says.
Never *DOWNS*. But sometimes, *UPS, NO*.
I think spring has been over a long time.
One day, the leaves smell of things dying.

Anecdote Of The Commonplace

One night the leaves smell of things dying
so sharply my legs begin jigs and two-steps,
trying to forget how my body aches with cold.

I clear the world of dreams and wake
in a bare-bones place where leaves shrivel on the ground,
going nowhere.

Oblong insects with more legs than any journey
eat the cabbage and upset all plans for wintering through. The pumpkin
has forgotten which holiday it stands for and goes sagging back to earth.

This air does not speak in parables. It clearly explains what we have:
normal, everyday suffering. No transmigrations here.
Even the birds have forgotten *south*, along with other names for shelter.

I am trying my best not to obscure things and have my rituals
of raking leaves. Songs of renewal catch me off-guard;
nothing could be more difficult than this.

If I told you of a tree fat with birds, singing fruit and the first spring,
would you believe me? Do you know, as you weed the garden,
only the weeds will come back?

Or when the moon whispers of rare harvests, do you understand its lies? And claim them, the way whole sheaves of birds chime in when one bird sings.

A Sort of Spring Song

One bird sings, keeping the day company, and me,
though I can't make out the words,
and recall the older movie actress, interviewed,
who asked, "Would you like to meet my dog?"
Her love is not to be doubted.
Whatever is lost in the folds of age,
the dog says it doesn't matter.
Says, "Feed me." Says, "The body still works magic;
its warmth is creature comfort, older than words."

I'm not saying this is wrong,
but I've always wanted the secrets things hold.
As I go to the creek,
trees are engulfing old wire fences, murmuring
to the ghosts of cows and small children.
I think they say, "Escape now. Life is short."
And also, "Watch out for the mud."

But this is not clear.
As I walk by the Indian pipes, jewel weed,
their mouths snap shut.
Either they keep their own council,
or—I sometimes think—they have been talking of me.

Their long stories would slowly make sense
of these patches in which, say,
the brown underbelly spores of Christmas fern
promise to last forever.

AGAINST THINGS

To last forever, someone I love tells me,
I must get inside of things.
I try to explain that I want out.
What business do things have running my life?

Driving downtown, I reach a sign that says *DO NOT PASS.*
Fine, I think, I will rot here,
and *rotting* comes so close I can feel my organs dream about decay.
Muscles fray slightly, longing to seep into some more vivid life.

All day the spiderweb between the bathroom mirror and scales clamors of
                                                                    gravity.
And a fingerprint on the wall convicts me again and again
of reading the daily news. These things collaborate, saying my name.
It never occurs to them to speak of themselves.

Only sometimes, I awake from a reverie I can't remember,
less of a *coming to* than a *might have been.*
At such times, I know among the scatter of car keys, receipts, and dust,
is everything I've ever lost.

CLONING

Everything I've ever lost returns to *tsk* at me like a maiden aunt.
Earrings and house keys jostle lost friends, lost faith,
and are joined by a few things that shouldn't be my problem:
a single shoe on the highway, a stray grocery cart.
Outside my window a bird sings, luring the neighborhood cat,
courting disaster. He doesn't know what you court, you get.

This, then, is the challenge: to live a decent life.
What desire could be sharper than this?
My aunt tells me she wants to be cloned, to escape being alone.
I set her and the endangered bird at odds,
avoiding an argument with myself. Together,
the four of us find happiness. We swing

from elegies to elegant nonsense, and practice dying falls.
We settle down and make ourselves at home.
We find we enjoy the shopping; we always return the carts.

LOST SOULS

Returning grocery carts, lost wallets, too much change,
I try to imagine the world comes to good.
It's like money in the bank, saved.

Our neighbors wanted to save the world.
Their born-again son, John, joined the army.
He came home horny and angry, an all-American boy.

Coveting me and my sisters, he betrayed what he found good
while we fed his desires, cousins to our own,
the way we fed monkeys in the zoo, unknowing and careless.

We had no idea what we wanted. It was easier when I was ten
and made lists of things I'd do. For instance, "sleep under stars."
It must have been the words I loved. The idea of night,

which changed one night when John threw rocks at our window
until darkness came spilling in.
For days, stars were trapped in the house.

Points of light would bump against us like bottom feeders;
what we'd wished upon had come too close.
We were in over our heads.

These days, I try not to rise to bait.
The grocery store may profit. I think for John
and stars and night and maybe even words, it's far too late.

HUM-DRUM DAYS

It's late, and daylight ends early.
Outside, everything smells of winter;
the forsythia has abandoned its leaves, leans
against the window, pointing in.
The empty clothesline's taut.
We are clearly waiting for something.

I want to give you the expectancy of this day
in which nothing
keeps arriving, beautifully,
in the gray variations of north.

Just imagine each morning
someone you love makes you oatmeal
and fills a thermos with tea.
Set on the dining room table,
it hisses small thermos songs
in harmony
with the furnace, wind, and pipes.
You can hear the hum in hum-drum.
It's all you needed to know.

LOOKING FORWARD TO LOOKING BACK

"I call you by name . . .
You will have stopped revolving except in crystal."
—Wallace Stevens

All we needed to know would come in a flash.
"Come the revolution," we said,
"We'll all have oysters and champagne."
We rowed the dinghy into the bay;

from rock, we pried loose creatures
so fresh they cringed at the sight of lemon.
The champagne was a different story,
which I'm not going to tell you.

But here: a young woman does an impromptu dance,
spinning, adding her colors to a bright seashore spring.
Two men watch her, glaring at each other.
This is no revolution, but we don't know that yet.

Desire lights the stars like candles
and serves the moon on half shells, tasting
of the effervescence of the sea. The revolution comes
and goes. The ocean comes and goes;

the sea, a soft-bodied animal between its two shores,
rolls back into itself. These days, my vocation is calling
to it. I want also to know
how Penelope spun out her days the second time

her man left, heading inland, to a country
where people live wholly on bread, and alone.
From here, there is no looking back,
and coming home is no great shakes.

The Pleasures Of Merely Re-circulating

Coming home is no great shakes.
Whatever happened to *going somewhere*?
The years used to be an education.
Now, we greet spring like a friend so old
there's nothing to say except "I'm here."

I'm here in a town with two main streets, Union and Grand;
each is one way, and opposite.
The trucks come and go, trading this for that.
I see in their repeated motions the evenings,
how I practice grand finales for mornings' reunions with the rain.

All night the gutters make rude noises, recycling rain.
Sometimes I know I could be anywhere;
sometimes I think this is untrue. For instance,
New Orleans' high school teachers have weekly duties—
homeroom, detention, and the alligator shift.

They watch young men and women behind the school
feeding cigarettes to the water when the teacher patrols.
No alligators anywhere in sight. Smoke loiters in the air;
it leaves traces of thin dreams, of cars or gin.
Nothing to write home about.

Meanwhile on Union a diesel turns the corner.
There's smoke on fog on rain.
Only later the sun comes out on a world so clean and
shaken by the light, the diesel sounds like a good idea.
It asks us to follow and, suckers that we are,
we say we will.

ROSARIES

Ambitio, Latin: a going round (for votes)

We say we will be home by ten,
and for once we are,
borrowing this night each other's bodies,

                     and returning them as good as new.
Next morning, next door, the grass is, as usual, greener.
Just so, on occasion, I have brief affairs
with the world.
              I read, thinking of roses,
"Plant Releases Toxic Fumes." I know this is a bad joke, but I keep reading:
"Tomato Threatens St. Louis." Tornadoes clear the back forty
all the while;
              I stand here, as if untouched,
ambitious as a politician who knows *ambition*
comes from Rome, from *going round.*
Only my canvas is smaller,
                  as we take our morning walk.
A man in a yellow car has bumped into a man in a pickup.
They exchange words and numbers in the heat.
Like theirs, our fires refuse to go out,
                   imagining a crisper air.
Today I mistrust such imagination, false promises. Why,
when I say *fire*, should I choose between *hearth* and *ardor*,
or think of persistent exchange?

16

                    I want to speak honestly
of white sales and pork chops. To say, on our walk,
here is that old man with his dog again,
coming back round like an old bone.
                                        I worry.
How will the man in the yellow car get home?
Although it will not make the headlines,
this is the daily news:
                    our walks, our bodies,
all homebodies, graying, alive according to a calendar
which divides one day from the next like a string of days,
on which we count
                    our luck.

Coming Up For Air

Our luck in still being here is amazing, though we say this in different ways.
In the city, men with sleeping bags curl up next to dumpsters
or line up for unwanted blessings and soup. Restless,

they've chalked their names on every south-bound freight.
I'm heading south too, toward the grocery store.
Along the freeway, names appear on rocks: Deano, Tim, and Val were here.

In rock, they still cruise the back roads making love in Fords.
At the railroad crossing, I start humming an old song
with the line, "You take what you need and you leave the rest."

Lumber, grain, and the homeless pass by. This is not the life of adventure.
Nor is it my life. I sing, half forgetting the words,
but I make up nothing. In a boxcar that says it serves the public

coast to coast: two men and a woman; they seem to have a dog.
They are waving; they are singing as they leave town.
The men's faces are all winter, craggy, and sharp.

This could be Tim and Deano. Val starts a song—of ironing,
of shopping, of how we all break bread. The men hum,
"This life is for the birds." Val's song imagines children,

in harmony; the three are singing rounds now,
the notes bobbing up and down, though the two men get off
beat and don't quite end where she begins.

Spring Cleaning

She begins again, trying to renew her life
as if it were a library book she kept meaning
to read. New carpets and reupholstered chairs
sprout in her rooms. Old correspondence is raked up,
turned over and burnt like leaves. The study is in order,
alphabetical. This is spring in the air.

Inner life, she thinks, is not renewable except by chance.
For instance, the moon at sunset after rain winks
like a lover promising a night so slowly filled
that *desire* becomes a forgotten word. Or more puzzling,
there are walks through gardens and cut lawns
that make smell the only sense to count.

But the new chairs also uphold the spirit.
If she squints, the fabrics sink into weeks of use
where she sits reading. Or dreams of refurnishing
yet again, polishing the floors, the lamps,
the very birds outside the window until she acquires
the knack of being at home.

MISS MARSHALL'S DARK NIGHT

At home and no one talking; only lethargy visits.
Only the power of lists. Some days she writes:
Get up. Take shower.
Later: *Wash right leg. Left.*
On a good day almost everything gets done.

When she leaves, the sun lights up the lilacs,
half-furred cones of white. A thug of a robin
patrols the good neighbors' fence. Meanwhile,
Miss M. talks to road conditions en route
to the post office. A woman with a walker

complains of being trapped in an old house.
At her local, later, the man in the next booth
wishes he had eaten. Time is knocked for a
loop, but evenings still come and go,
senseless as an insomniac's chant.

If her town had sunrises, she would welcome them
in place of this slow rising of sight. If the town had silence,
she might sleep, abandon these hours listening to trucks
strain up grades, the freight yard's heavy couplings,
the house crumbling so slowly you hardly catch time's drift.

GETTING AWAY FROM IT ALL

Drifting without a language,
how do you memorize a place not your own?
A five-member band demonstrates:

blind man on the organ; his wife—
unaware she's gained thirty pounds—
grins at the one-note drummer.

Two others do nothing. They all
play for tips. Behind them the cooler
says "Nestlé. Bambino."

Fishing boats litter the harbor. Cats
prowl around the melon leaning
on one wall. The wall insists we all

vote for the mayor: Gerardo.
Although everyone knows what will
come to pass, they must *Vota Asi.*

The band passes a tambourine
and talks as the coins play a tune
the blind man knows by heart.

SPRING'S ETERNAL

The blind man knows by memory's touch what is *carnal*
is of the spirit. As in bed lovers turn, pivoting
on a fulcrum and the world moves. Archimedes turns
in his grave—so simple, why did he not see instinctively

the way spouses read the unwashed dishes in the sink.
They say "I'll take care of it." What they mean is:
"This is not what I want." In the language mothers use.
My mother's life was never what she wanted although, wanting,

her life was full: each day a celebration of need, articulate,
signifying something just out of reach. I think about my mother,
going after what I can hold. As in gardening, which is like tobacco,
which is habit-forming: there's always one more weed.

It's one damn thing after another in the index of my days.
The entries read: "Domesticity." Or "Knowledge," with a subentry:
"Galileo, Imagined away friction." After a night of love and dishes,
I spade the ground: the earth moves.

GROUND CONTROL

The world moves without
our descriptions.
Or so they say.
Tongues flap and never
get off the ground.

When I fought the water company,
I was articulate; privileged, I knew
the language bureaucrats salute,
and ran it up their
flagpole. Things moved

fast enough then
though the water went off
next door. Fluent in some language
we say we *have* English; we do
or don't *have* Spanish.

Though I resolve to pocket nothing
this time around, I find I have:
ticket stubs, old kleenex,
the loud irritating voice
of a neighbor who sells houses.

And I remember a childhood walk
to a lake. In a tarpaper shack
on the way, the three bears lived.
My father said so and so
I believed, treading carefully

although the posted signs
on the door were from a public
utility. The bears had their uses too—
I never approached the lake alone.
It seems our stories take flight:

I argue with the company
and the bears lose everything,
to say nothing of my neighbors—real
estate or other. Their lives seep into mine
like fluid speech seeking its own level.

THE INNER MAN

He levels charges at winter
which does some leveling of its own.
Choruses used to sing in the empty furrows;
his mother's clothespin bag fraying
on the line hummed along with the birds.

Now whole days slip out the back door.
He's arrested for not paying attention.
For example, nothing comes to mind.
Dead ends pile up on the compost heap
like all the things he might have been.

Here is where the snow should arrive
to repossess the landscape. There should be
snow angels, snow men, and newer
creatures for whom there are no words.
Instead, this ice age begins in rain.

The fathering is over. As spring comes,
he will mother himself—praise
fingers, belly, feet, the parts
that work hard daily, hungering
for praise, of what is, solicitous.

THE PASSION FOR IMITATION TRIES

to solicit
equal affection for what
is a delight:
the man in the Pharmacy
Diner on Spruce
Street—where the waitress is
called Mary—handing your
order over from
the grill, saying "One toasted
English: here you

are sweetheart," without offense even
in a diner
in summer. Russell claimed that
to reach the core
of scientific truth one
must oust what is
purely verbal, and this
from a man who also said a hat tumbling
off in a mirror does so
out of passion.

THEATERS OF OPERATION

"[not] to stir into poems baseball or Bo Diddly"
—Robert Pinsky

Seeing passion's not ruled by the moon
but by the stars, I pucker my lips and whistle.
Raised in the passion pit, I say "I love Cary Grant
with all my heart." Or sometimes, half-hearted
and embarrassed, I consider surgeons and love
open-heartedly. Think of clean white squares
framing a muscled heart that squats like a frog
in a bio lab. Or think of two hearts beating as one.
Whose heart is this anyway? Does it matter?

Masses of hearts beat out the rhythms
of things that come back, seasonal as hormones
but homier—like taking the dog for a walk.
The trick is to move but imagine nothing that sticks
in the mind like a Madison Avenue line. Neither is the dog
disposable. Though he's gone, I still stumble over him
like a phantom limb or a word in a language that's lost.
Combining calm with passion, a heart suffers whatever
it's thrown, like my old dog with his daily round.

I say I hate this knowing what comes next with a passion—
but whose? We're all in this together, growing older,
and entropy's in the stars, they say. So it's a question
of what moves me as I try to stake out a life
worthy of someone. Even the surgeon walks his dog.
Under a lamp post he meets Cary Grant or his neighbor.
Does it matter which one? They are all men of action.

HEARING VOICES

"We're both men of action."
The person behind me forecasts his life:
"We'll meet again in foreign parts."
I inspect the tall dark strangers as they pass.

What company I keep. Or not company, collections.
These pieces of overheard conversation—like facts
for which we have no explanation.
What we need is a physics of casual exchange.

More often physics tells you why, when you jump in a rowboat,
a gun goes off. And how long this takes.
These things of interest as the clutter of our days;
the aesthetic of unthinking, minds unraveling like hems

or lines cast over and over and catching nothing—
language run amok with no feeling.
But there is a feeling here:
the restless blank in which we mostly live.

And the question of why there is no poetry of this.
I am talking about growing up or old,
the voices that retreat, or say less,
that haunt less even as the objects of our fear approach.

STILL LIFE

Approaching the end of the line, the train
has six passengers left. Two ten-year-old girls
are still excited, having crept onto a balcony
to watch "Cleopatra." They hardly mention the movie,

more taken with the thrill of climbing illicit stairs
to lie together in the dark, heads down to escape
being caught, hormones clattering for more
though they don't know of what.

The mother of the family opposite them knows
it's been a hard day. Her baby fills the train
with screams while the father stares at one wall
as if he's doing a study of defacement, as if

he never before saw the woman who takes his child
from him; he looks surprised to find himself
grown up to be a man in transit here
in this brawl of train, giggle, bawling,

and the brooding ill humor of the woman,
louder than all the noises and voices that overlap
like geometric planes. If this were a photograph,
I'd be the older woman in the corner.

Part of me is wondering what to buy for dinner;
part of me imagines the train, just as grubby as it is now,
coming back from the round house, empty,
after we've found our stations and gone on our way.

THE WAY HE OR SHE SEES IT

The way she looked at him was the way he looked
at the pear tree in the back yard, blossoms just open,
against the further back pines. This is serious,

when you start eyeing the landscape with something
like lust. You start to wonder:
What do we want? Here it's all

snap-shots, moments where colors seem more
of the mind than of the world, but startlingly
distanced—insistent. Like two would-be lovers

recognizing at a party stark need
and excitement, promising there's no mistake,
no one will say that's not what I mean.

No one will say anything.
Not even *pear tree, pine.* Or *white, pink, green.* It's
as if the world could melt and re-form. But of course

it won't. We don't live happily ever after the way
the pictures have it. Somebody usually gets up the next
morning; somebody pays the rent and makes the bed.

The dishes remain to be done, always. And the pears
will come and go and come back. There's more than one
problem in figure and ground:

Is this a story about a woman who wants so much
she makes the party—the bad wine, crackers, and cheese—
disappear? Are we discussing how, lips slightly parted, two people

speak the same tongue? It's a classic image: one slow wink
and you have a cup, running over perhaps. The way
the world, sometimes, runs wild in a riot of fruit, color,

or change. If you close both eyes, now, you'll see yourself
looking at a picture of a man and a woman or a cup. In a minute
you'll get up and wash the dishes or start dinner or eat.

FAMILIARITY

Eating was what my grandmother
peddled. So she had more to hold
against us. Brandishing cold cuts

and cakes, her own plate was
cottage cheese, lettuce, and one
unnaturally flesh-colored pear.

The pear spoke volumes
but looked like an ear
attentive to whatever curdling

could be arranged. Her children
still start if touched, and mistrust
or envy familiarity.

Like the man who handles names
with ease: "Well [insert name],"
he says, "it's been a pleasure."

He has the personal
touch, with my grandmother
shares a coercive art.

"We were all in different parts
of the house reading," I read
from a poet who confused the body

of his work with the body
of the world, of parts of the world,
say, of the soft envelope of flesh

behind his wife's left ear,
a place so private and lonely
it has no name. It is a space

the right shape for someone's lips.
We do feed on others. I try to stop
reading biographies. They all end

the same way: pared down
like a family credo, hard to decline,
compelling, compulsory.

BIOLOGY LESSON

"Compulsory attendance," he tells each year's
biology class but he means he wants
them to love him. They joke about excuses—
the dog ate my homework—but in his dreams
even the dogs trot their bones in on time.

All his skeletons are out of the closet
and at work. Mondays are like family
reunions. When the kids bother him at home
he's on top of the world; humming for weeks,
he accompanies himself down the hall.

Looking at themselves in the restrooms,
his classes never try to see him looking back.
But his pen is coveted: a woman, face
bland as a chalkboard, lives in his breast
pocket; as he writes, her evening gown slides

down the pen like a ship capsizing in slow motion,
all hands on deck. This could be an image
of writing and desire. Or of biology: how we become
what the billboards advise. Just as the students
want the pen because they think they should.

Sometimes, when his pen's not out, they imagine
the woman's body disappears murmuring *tibia,*
femur, carpus. And then the skeleton joins
the act, its structured outline sinking to new
depths, until the last fingertip is gone.

But he's not a man of such vision.
There's been no mistake. This is someone
who loves his work and makes his living,
each day joined to the next, no end in sight,
except the one required of us all.

Exercise For The Heart

We all try to love our neighbors despite the litanies of
                                        children
who won't come in to eat or the real estate woman out
                                        jogging
through the last warm days of fall. The elders pace,
                                        waiting for
the world to get on with its end, and watching over their neighbors'
                                        homes.

My lights are trained to go on as I go out so
                                        the burglars
can see too.   Daily the leaves whisper *loss* and
                                        tired of it,
sending garbled signals of distress. Wise in their ways,
I can read the signs.   But where do I
                                        go from here—

Here small changes make each day count. It matters if
                                        the hybrid rose has died,
whether the enlisted son will come home on furlough to sit
                                        at the bay window
and assemble model ships. The smaller children hover like
                                        vultures, knowing
after the ships fill the sailor's time, he will get rid of them.
                                        Just as

the navy will get rid of him, a fate for which he might be
practicing
though he doesn't know this. There's no virtue in knowing. Knowing
doesn't
make me love the sailor, though I wish I could, giving in
turn
what I would be given, as if the world were a class
act.

Meanwhile physics is busy disapproving: much *is* lost,
they say,
though they don't mean losing the way I do; on the topic
of loss,
I find other sciences sound better. Still, physics can't surprise an
absent heart,
growing heavy and foolish even as I try to keep it in
practice at home.

WHAT TO DO

—for Judith

In practice, we are at home with ourselves
whatever we might think. Displacement is just
difference in position. Let there be light,
God said and—a moment later, light travelling
as it does—there was. No surprise.

When I pack to travel, it takes longer:
where will the iron fit? What of packing lists?
Or weight limits? Should I bring lunch?
I love the poet who insists we imagine
the literal. But one can go too far.

A friend once drove with me to an empty mansion.
Imagine, she said, *the butler brings you tea.*
I'm with her; I'm having two lumps and milk.
She: *Your silk nightgown is lovely.*
I look down. I see my old terry robe

will shock the servants. I must go home and pack.
At this rate I'll never get away, occupied

with what to wear or how to get finches out of the eaves.
It's a child-like vision, but this child's writing letters:
I'm fine; today I washed my hair.

If this seems too light-hearted a way
to say good-bye, it's because I'm travelling
light. Any body could. I check my schedule:
Eyes. Ears. Hands. Feet. All packed. I know
how to do this part. I'm all set. I'll write.

NAUTICAL GESTURE

"To recall a name you've forgotten, try reciting the
alphabet. When you get to the letter with which the
name begins, it will spring to mind."
—Household Hints

Writing letters, paying bills: the morning is not promising.
She spends her time rummaging through the alphabet
for the names of friends she's misplaced. She's never cultivated
vagueness, but resents it when a neighborhood lawn edger hauls her back
from loss like an early phone call shearing off a dream.

My friends mock me for answering the phone with "this is she,"
as if my name arrived, a stranger I slowly recognize
and ask in so we can discuss old times. Dallying
with memories, she and I sail through a day that rights itself
like a ship coming in, riding low with a cargo of odds and ends,

and bearing good news. I mention the ship only to tide me over;
it's a vehicle that can't carry too much weight. I was really speaking
of things more pedestrian—writing letters, getting lost in unfamiliar
daydreams, the way what's lost can sometimes be called home
by sheer repetition of speech.

SIGNS OF THE TIMES

Speaking of what we do everyday, she asks what things have come to
when buying new shoes serves to vary the days. She means "Who am I?"
Shoes used to be for going places. Now her specialty is coming home.
Or she is home and everything else is leaving. Look: no birds, the fire's out,
and the wind has shifted—north.

The idea was to settle, like a dog circling its place of sleep, into routine:
cleaning the closet, shopping at a store that holds under one roof
shoes and books and food. The town drunk, Dirty Dan, is back on his
                                                            street corner
waiting for the aliens to give him a sign. She tries for signs too,
but from what is familiar.

The local shop door says "While exiting, if alarm sounds, please return."
Or: "While exciting . . . " It doesn't matter, she thinks as she exits,
                                                misreading all the signs.
Today Dirty Dan gives her a quarter. "Buy the paper," he says. "Watch.
Read with care." And she does. Sometimes she goes back over the years
hoping they will teach her

how to live well, like a book of days, remaindered. Like Dan,
always on the look out for trouble, she checks each dog-eared page.
Wants an adventure. Something to mark time. But not to waste it, to keep
the rhythms even of the worst days sounding out. And not in
preparation for flight.

About the Author

Lisa Malinowski Steinman is also the author of *Lost Poems* (Ithaca House, 1976), *All That Comes To Light* (Arrowood Books, 1989), and of a critical study, *Made In America: Science, Technology, and American Modernist Poets* (Yale University Press, 1987). Her work has received recognition from the Rockefeller Foundation, the National Endowment for the Arts, and the National Endowment for the Humanities. She is Professor of English and Humanities at Reed College in Portland, Oregon.

OTHER BOOKS BY LISA M. STEINMAN

LOST POEMS
Ithaca House, 1976

❖ ❖ ❖

*MADE IN AMERICA: SCIENCE, TECHNOLOGY,
AND AMERICAN MODERNIST POETS*
Yale University Press, 1987

❖ ❖ ❖

ALL THAT COMES TO LIGHT
Arrowood Books, 1989

❖ ❖ ❖

OTHER TITLES FROM ARROWOOD BOOKS

WINTER INSOMNIA
poems by Joseph Powell

❖ ❖ ❖

ALL THAT COMES TO LIGHT
poems by Lisa M. Steinman

❖ ❖ ❖

SORROWFUL MYSTERIES
stories by Normandi Ellis

❖ ❖ ❖

THE LIGHT STATION ON TILLAMOOK ROCK
a poem by Madeline DeFrees

❖ ❖ ❖

YELLOW
poems by Anne Pitkin

❖ ❖ ❖

DEADLY VIRTUES
a novel by François Camoin

❖ ❖ ❖

NORTHWEST VARIETY
essays edited by Lex Runciman and Steven Sher

❖ ❖ ❖

CHRISTMAS AT THE JUNIPER TAVERN
a play by Charles Deemer

❖ ❖ ❖

LUCY AND THE BLUE QUAIL
a poem by Lee Bassett

❖ ❖ ❖

Available from your local bookstore, or write for ordering information:
Arrowood Books, P.O. Box 2100, Corvallis, Oregon 97339

Colophon

A Book of Other Days is typeset in 10 point Lucida condensed,
with titles in 14 point small capitals.